Uncle Max came for a visit. He brought presents for Biff, Chip and Kipper.

"These shells are from the other side of the world," he told them.

The children always loved to hear Uncle Max's stories.

When they were ready for bed, he agreed to tell them all about his latest adventures.

"Since I last saw you, I have been looking for adventure on the high seas," Uncle Max began.

"What happened?" asked Kipper. "What did you see? Was it dangerous?"

"Well, one time I went for a swim and was surrounded by huge stinging jellyfish," Uncle Max smiled. "Do you know what I did?"

"Not really," said Kipper.

"I had a brilliant idea!" said Uncle Max. "I pulled out a spoon and shouted, 'Yum, yum! Jelly for tea!' All the jellyfish swam off when they heard that!"

"Wow," said Biff. "But why did you
have a spoon with you?"

"You never know when you might need
a spoon," said Uncle Max.

"Another time a hungry shark wanted to
eat me when I was diving for treasure," he
continued. "So do you know what I did?"
"I'm not sure," said Kipper.

"Luckily, I had *another* brilliant idea," said Uncle Max. "I scared that shark off with a sword."

"You had a *sword* with you?" asked Biff in surprise.

"Not a real sword," said Uncle Max.
"There was a swordfish swimming past, so
I used that!"

"Wow!" said Kipper.

"Is that possible?" asked Chip.

"You'd be surprised what can happen at sea," Uncle Max said. "Once I . . ."

He stopped and pointed at the light in the corner. "Why is that key glowing?" he asked.

"It does that when it's taking us on an adventure," said Biff.

Uncle Max had no time to ask any more questions. The magic took them all away.

It took them to a little boat in the middle
of the sea.

Uncle Max looked at the water all
around them.

"What on earth's going on?" he asked.

The children told him all about the magic key.

"We go on lots of exciting adventures," said Biff.

"Just like you, Uncle Max," said Kipper.

A dark shape passed under the boat. It wasn't just big. It was *enormous*.

"What was that?" asked Chip nervously.

"Um . . . I'm not sure," said Uncle Max.

A huge whale's tail burst out of the water.
It towered high above them.

"Come on, Uncle Max," said Kipper.
"You must have a brilliant idea to escape!"

Before Uncle Max could answer, the enormous tail slapped down on the water right next to the boat. Splash!

It made a huge wave that carried the boat away.

The boat zoomed off, riding along the
top of the wave.

"This is just like one of your stories,
Uncle Max!" shouted Chip.

Uncle Max gripped the sides of the boat.

Another huge shape rose from the water
in front of them.

"An even *bigger* whale!" shouted Biff.

"Have you got a brilliant idea yet,
Uncle Max?" Kipper asked.

"Not just yet," said Uncle Max.

He didn't have time to say anything else.
The whale's open mouth was like a huge
cave and they were rushing towards it.

"Hold on tight!" shouted Biff.

The boat rushed into the whale's enormous mouth, along with seawater, seaweed and lots of silver fish. Everything went dark.

They stopped in a big, gloomy place.
"We must be in the whale's tummy!"
said Biff.

Uncle Max looked around and shook his
head. "That's not possible," he said. "*Is it?*"

Kipper gave Uncle Max a hopeful look.
"How about now?" he asked. "Any
brilliant ideas for how to get out?"

"No!" groaned Uncle Max. He looked
soggy and miserable.

For a long time the only noise was the gurgling of the whale's tummy.

Suddenly Uncle Max jumped up. "Wait! I *have* got an idea," he shouted, "and it's a *brilliant* one!"

He began to rock the boat from side
to side.

"Join in!" he told the children. "If we
do it enough, I'm sure it will make the
whale burp!"

There was a rumbling noise all around.
"I think it's working!" said Kipper.

Biff gripped the sides of the boat. "We'd better hold on tight again," she said.

Just then Biff spotted a bright light.
The magic key was glowing, at last.

"Don't worry," she said. "There's a much
easier way out of here!"

The next moment they all were safely back in Biff's bedroom.

Uncle Max blinked. He looked around the room, rubbed his eyes and blinked again. He scratched his head.

"Sorry, children," he said. "I think I fell asleep for a moment. I had the *strangest* dream!"

Biff slipped the magic key into her pocket.

Uncle Max noticed something.
"How on earth did this tiny bit of
seaweed get on my sleeve?" he asked.
The children glanced at each other
and grinned.

Uncle Max held the seaweed between his fingers.

"Actually, this reminds me of the time I had a tickling competition with a giant octopus," he said.

"Wow! That sounds amazing," said Biff. "What did you do?"

"Luckily I had a brilliant idea," said Uncle Max. "Can you guess what?"

"Not really," said Kipper happily.

"Well," said Uncle Max, "earlier that day
I had made friends with an electric eel..."
The children snuggled down to enjoy one
more tall tale before bedtime.